To Mrs. G——

my Best Wishes

Mary G. King

Weathered wood with flowers

Weathered wood

with flowers by Mary G. Knight

William Morrow & Company, Inc.
425 Park Avenue South • New York N.Y. 10016

For my patient husband

CONTENTS

FOREWORD

by Helen Van Pelt Wilson, Editor

One of the pleasures of being an editor—and there are many—is the opportunity to watch talents grow. In the years when I regularly prepared a calendar for Barrows, I looked forward to the package of photographs that came from Mary Knight. Her pictures were always of first quality, clear and well lighted; as a perfectionist, she saw to this. But it was her increasingly handsome designs that produced such delight.

Her compositions were never of a set kind. She read widely and experimented constantly so that various traditions and many styles affected her work. Yet all was assimilated. Her arrangements were inevitably her own, even when we recognized the inspiration of a Flemish bouquet or a Japanese nageire. And her enthusiasms have widened and changed; this is one of the great charms of her designing.

This book on weathered wood represents a long-time interest in which her point-of-view as to the ways of using wood has gradually altered. Today it is only rarely accessory to a design. Mrs. Knight now makes weathered wood the dominant element. This attitude has resulted in compositions of great charm and originality so that whatever our personal taste may be, we find here many arresting studies to excite our imagination—and admiration.

ABOUT
WEATHERED WOOD

Wood, shaped and seasoned by nature, has interested me for years. But, like other designers, I used what we originally called driftwood in fairly pedestrian ways— as background for wall plaques decorated with dried flowers and cones, as part of a naturalistic scene in which figures of woodland creatures were far more important than the fallen log or make-believe tree.

Today the intrinsic qualities of what we now call weathered wood are what I find so attractive. The various shapes; the different patinas of wood resulting from the action of sun, wind, and water; the rhythm of the grain, all these are stimulating to the creative designer. Even one piece of wood can be the basis for innumerable designs with flowers, fruits, and foliages—fresh, dried, or painted—or stand almost alone as sculpture.

What I have learned as the essential in working with

weathered wood is that the wood must predominate. Before any design is considered, the qualities of the wood must be "seen," and then these qualities must be permitted to dominate, whether in flower-show pieces or home decorations. When emphasis is so placed, almost inevitably the resulting design has distinction.

In the preparation of this book, I have had the good fortune to work with skilled photographers, and to have as well the encouragement and assistance of many good friends, all of whom I cannot mention here by name, but I should like to express my thanks specifically:

To these three most helpful photographers—Lewis Henderson, Jr., and also Ted Walls for the black-and-white pictures; David Vargo, C.P.P., of Carpenter's Studio for the color.

To Frank S. Curto, Horticulturist of Phipps Conservatory in Pittsburgh, and to Kate Clapp of the Akron *Beacon Journal* for identification of certain plant materials.

To Lucille Parry for her encouragement, generosity, and helpfulness in bringing me treasures of weathered wood from Florida; to Margaret Lang for contributing a beautiful, and enormous, hornet's nest, as well as wood from her own collection; to Mae Steinbach for the railroad ties I made into bases.

And I am again most grateful to Cynthia C. Luden for her painstaking editorial preparation of this manuscript.

Cuyahoga Falls, Ohio   Mary G. Knight
March, 1968

Weathered wood with flowers

I

Where to find

weathered wood

To those of us who design with wood, the term "driftwood" is no longer descriptive of the great variety of wood in use today, for it suggests only those pieces that have floated on the tides and been cast up on banks and beaches. Designers are now collecting wood forms—limbs, trunks, stumps, and roots —that have been exposed to sun, rain, snow, water, and wind. Some of it has been gnawed by animals or hammered by birds or tunneled by insects. Some has been bleached or stained by earth or sand, some rubbed and polished by pebbles, or carved by rock. So we use the term "weathered

1

wood" to suggest the multiplicity of nature's means of creating these masterpieces of wood.

You can search them out almost any place except in a concrete city block. Wherever shrubs and trees grow, pieces of wood bearing the marks of weather can be found. A good time to search is following a storm after strong winds have uprooted decayed trees and torn off dead limbs.

A holiday may take you to an isolated area where wood has been lying on the ground undisturbed for years. A sharp eye will locate desirable pieces on mountains, hillsides, in woods, along lakes, streams, rivers, and beaches, and even in the desert. Some intriguing forms may turn up near dams, reservoirs, and streams where the water-level changes considerably. Roots no longer part of living trees, alternately exposed to hot sun and submerged in water, take on compelling shapes and colors. And where construction is underway for housing, roads, and highways, great earthmovers expose all kinds of weathered wood. What variety there is—strong and weak, delicate and heavy, light or dark, single compact forms, many-sectioned pieces, curved or straight, with grain moving first one direction then another—and no two pieces alike.

Because so many people are collecting, some places seem to have been picked clean, especially certain seashore and resort areas.

However, these are just the places where little road side gift shops frequently sell unusual pieces of weathered wood, some already treated or rubbed to a glowing patina. And hobby suppliers and florist shops in your own area may carry weathered wood. So if you find yourself empty-handed near the end of a vacation or collecting trip, check the shops nearby before you leave; you probably won't return home without a few new pieces to spur you on to fresh creative designing.

2

I find the joy of collecting and the thrill of discovery are part of the satisfaction of working with wood, and even my own backyard has yielded a treasure or two.

1   Bunches of artificial black, green, and purple grapes
        and clusters of dried golden yarrow richly adorn this
        single piece of gray wood from Pennsylvania. Scotch
        broom, also dried, adds a lively flourish. Plant
        materials are placed in crevices, and the fruit draped
        to hang down from the upper section. A metal
        dowel secures the wood in this horizontal position.

2   A mottled purple-red root section, cast up by excavation for a housing development, is supported by a metal rod attached to a red-brown lamp base. Red roses and foliage are kept fresh in a cupholder on the base and in a plastic tube placed in a natural opening at the top.

3   Rhythmic ribbons of brown roots shaped naturally
into a bow and loops are combined with red, orange,
and yellow-shaded heliconias that look like carved
extensions of the wood. The pleasing relationship
between soft sprays of green Hawaiian pine and
brown patches of glaze on the Japanese ceramic
contributes textural contrast. A waxy red bromeliad
flashes hot color through the loop of wood on the
left.

8

4   This large section of gray-white wood from Assateague Island off the coast of Virginia calls for
bold design. Brilliant red gladiolus form the "shadow"
half of this compact upright. Green cut-philodendron, clipped to angular outline, and strands of
bleached Scotch broom increase the volumetric emphasis.

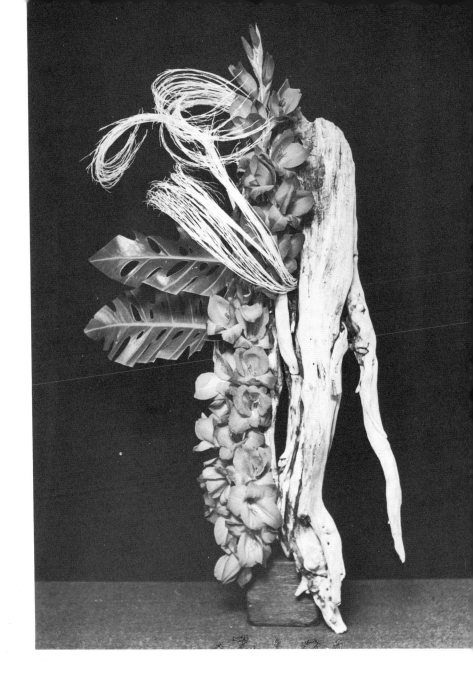

5   By extension of our theme, an orange lichen with tan rings that looks like a cross-section of tree trunk is material for designing. Drilled and held on a base of weathered railroad tie by a metal rod, the lichen disk provides a bright round foil for green foliages —the stalwart *Curculigo capitulata,* gleaming magnolia, and lacy redwood—with asphodel pods.

2

How to clean

and condition

Before I clean a piece of weathered wood, I first consider the value of the existing surface. If it is caked with dirt or coated with slime, it is not possible to judge until this is removed. But with a fairly dry piece, whose surface has been exposed, you can tell what you have. Subtle coloring or a pleasing patina could be destroyed by hasty scrubbing. Sometimes wind and sun polish a piece so clean that adding a few flowers or a bit of green foliage is all that is required to draw attention to the artistry of nature.

More often than not a fair amount of cleaning is necessary. Grooves and crevices may contain deposits of sand, decayed fungus, and such, or a colony of tiny creatures may still be in residence. My first step in cleaning is to spray the wood, while it is outdoors, with a strong jet from the garden hose. This removes surface soil and washes away any undesirables. Now it is easier to see what the surface is like. Next, to preserve color and texture, I scrub gently with a soft brush dipped in a solution of warm water and mild soap or detergent. A narrow bottle-brush is good for some crevices and an old toothbrush for others. Fine and heavy wire brushes easily remove imbedded particles.

Wood that requires more extensive cleaning can be scrubbed all over with wire brushes. This treatment will intensify the weathered look for, though surface coloration may disappear, the tones underneath are not likely to be disappointing. Grain is also enhanced by scrubbing and linear rhythms accented.

Any rotted or pulpy sections should be scraped out with a knife or sawed off, the areas then smoothed with fine sandpaper. Finally, spray with an insect repellent, let piece dry.

Sun-bleached surfaces can be restored by saturating the wood with water a number of times and letting it stand out in hot sun for weeks or through the whole summer. Damaged bark can be peeled from wet roots. If roots have dried out, soak them in hot water, then peel. Use a sharp knife on stubborn sections.

To remove bark from corkscrew or pussy willow branches, peel right after cutting and while they are still green. Treat wisteria, wild grape, and other vines and branches the same way. Otherwise soak and then peel. Not strictly weathered wood, these stripped materials associate well with it.

After cleaning, let wood dry thoroughly before treating it further. Always dry it out well before storing.

6   This handsome piece of weathered wood, found in Pennsylvania, received a good cleaning with a forceful spray of water, followed by a gentle scrubbing with soap and warm water. The soft gray wood, prominently placed, the shiny pink anthuriums kept fresh in water-filled plastic tubes, and one glossy green cut-philodendron leaf combine, with dramatic lighting, to make an emphatic statement.

7   Baroque rhythms in the grain of this gray wood
     from Lake Erie were enhanced by a thorough clean-
     ing with wire brushes. Seen as an extension of the
     wood are the red-violet cattleya orchids in plastic
     tubes. Skeletonized cactus leaves, painted black, are
     pinned to the wood for lacy contrast; the polished
     base lends formality—and support.

     18

8   To preserve the soft gray-brown patina of this elegant form, scrubbing was omitted; the only cleaning, a good hosing down with water. To emphasize the wood, with its delicate linear surface detail and subtle shaping, materials are limited to three crisp rounds of Queen-Anne's-lace and a tall, black-painted spiral of weed.

20

3

Methods

of treatment

Natural wood, weathered and worn, makes a direct and honest statement that appeals to us. But occasionally we want to experiment. We try to emphasize the twist of a root by removing as much color as possible, or we are bold and paint an extraordinary shape black—or even red. Where sections of wood have been joined to make one piece, we often apply paint to unify the form. We discover that certain stains and waxes can enhance, without noticeably changing, the essential qualities of a handsomely weathered piece.

BLEACHING

To bleach wood, soak it for an hour or so in equal parts of household bleach and water. Then rinse carefully in fresh water. The wood will dry a warm honey tone. Bleaching may raise the grain. Rub with fine sandpaper to a smooth finish if you prefer it. For a whiter tone, soak wood in a stronger solution until you get the shade you want. It will always dry lighter.

Oxalic acid crystals bring a rosy hue to the bleached wood. You can buy these crystals in a drugstore. Simply combine an equal amount of crystals and water and treat the surface with the mixture.

To make such materials as ferns and Scotch broom compatible with treated wood, immerse them in a kettle of boiling bleach. If possible, do this outdoors on a windless day, or indoors with the windows open. The fumes can be toxic. Rinse in clear water, shape, and dry flat.

WAXING AND OILING

After a piece of wood has been bleached and sanded, you may want to give it a subtle sheen. Apply a self-polishing liquid wax and rub lightly to a glowing finish. This produces a somewhat sophisticated effect, appropriate for stylized designs.

Warm linseed oil will darken wood and can also be rubbed to a fine soft finish.

STAINING

Wood stains are available in shades of brown from cinnamon and mahogany to nutmeg and walnut. Brush a light coat on, let dry, and check the color. You can darken with a

23

second coat if you want to. Always let the wood dry between applications. Sand lightly after the stain is dry. Apply wax or linseed oil to increase the gleam. A varnish stain will give sheen to the wood.

PAINTING

When you paint driftwood, you alter it considerably. All but coarse textures are covered, as is the grain and, of course, the natural wood tones are lost. But there are occasions when the design you have in mind calls for a clear dramatic form. Paint will emphasize the form by eliminating surface detail.

If you join pieces of wood to create a new shape, the sections will probably have different tones, grains, and textures. To unify them you may want to paint the whole piece rather than bleach or stain it.

Wood with deep grooves and crevices is best spray-painted. Flat areas can be covered easily with a brush. Water-base paint, such as poster paints or Liquidtex, can be brushed on and areas wiped with a damp cloth for blending. You can wash off most of any water-soluble paint, but some color is likely to remain in crevices.

Painted wood is excellent for abstract designs and those with a strong element of fantasy.

CHALKING

To cover repairs on cut surfaces of wood, I use pastel chalks. If you have removed a branch or cut away decayed areas, the exposed part is usually a different tone. After sanding with fine sandpaper, try rubbing chalk lightly on the freshly cut surface. Blend it into the adjacent area. You may

24

I   In this design dominated by one bright red "patent-leather"
anthurium and a cluster of yellow-veined croton leaves, the term
weathered wood is extended to dried, peeled wisteria painted shiny
black. Shaped into scribbles and twists, the vine delineates spaces
that are partially occupied by two paler anthuriums. Stability for
the linear excitement is provided by the cylindrical volumes of the
off-white container by Edna Arnow.

II   Interlocking pussy willow, peeled and bleached, some of it
painted fluorescent orange and green, construct a linear frame for
two clusters of yellow viburnum berries with leaves and a stalk of
velvet red gladiolus. This sculpture of lines is supported in the
multiple openings of a contemporary ceramic by Canadian artist,
Aileen Hagell.

III   Roots from an osage orange tree cross and loop in rhythmical
diagonals from one spout of the Japanese ceramic. From the other
spout, rise masses of pointed pink-veined croton leaves. Chartreuse
allium heads—starry rounds displayed in space on straight stems—
provide delicate contrast.

IV Golden gloriosa daisies appear sophisticated in the company
of orange-painted teasels—in stiff horizontal and vertical place-
ments—a black-lacquered root formation, and exotic croton leaves.
Two sections of wood, attached by screws and unified by paint, are
braced by a metal rod thrust in a wooden block. A cupholder con-
tains water for the fresh materials.

need to use several shades to achieve a matching tone. (To avoid the unpleasantly dry feeling on my fingers, I wear cotton gloves for this operation.) Rub the wood with a soft cloth for final blending and to remove excess chalk.

For a soft overall color, rub the whole piece of wood with chalk. Textures remain and may thus be enhanced. You can apply a clear plastic spray to keep chalk from rubbing off.

FOR A BLUE-GREEN PATINA

To get an interesting, colorful surface, prepare a solution of : 1 cup clear (not soapy) ammonia, 2 tablespoons of copper powder (available at hardware, paint, or art-supply stores) and 2 to 3 tablespoons of white glue. Apply to the wood with a brush. After the mixture has oxidized, and the wood has dried, a lovely blue-green patina will appear. For a shade more green than blue, use more copper powder. This method of coloring wood does not conceal texture.

FOR AN ENCRUSTED WHITE SURFACE

A material called water glass, which chemically is sodium silicate in liquid form, can be bought from a drugstore. Brush this on areas where you want a crusty-white, barnacle-like texture. Burn with a propane torch. You may want to cover a whole piece of wood if the form is not too complex. More complicated pieces frequently look better if some areas are left untreated.

SANDBLASTING

To remove surface texture and color, have wood sand-blasted at a shop that refinishes furniture or at an automobile body-repair shop. A light tone and smooth finish will result.

9   A sparkling white surface can be devised by applying water glass—sodium silicate—to the wood with a brush and then burning with a propane torch. On simple forms, such as the one on the right, the entire surface can be treated to good effect. If some areas on more elaborate pieces are left untouched, the sense of depth will be increased.

26

10 A stout pine branch, nubs and twigs removed, provides a simple form suited to treatment with water glass. When burned with a propane torch, this substance forms a brilliant white bubbled crust. Variegated green-and-white dogwood and funkia foliages associate well with this texture, as does the bubbled glaze on the heavy Japanese ceramic. Vibrant blue-and-orange strelitzias inserted in an opening in the wood help to anchor it. All fresh materials are held in a needlepoint holder.

28

11   A rhythmic slab of wood, treated with clear ammonia, copper powder, and glue, provides a bluegreen upright for dusty pink Joe-Pye weed and white Queen-Anne's-lace, composed in a geometry of long hollow reeds. To stabilize the wood, an upside-down needlepoint holder is screwed into it and locked into another holder set right-side up in the bowl. A clinker from a coke furnace conceals both.

30

12   A branch of manzanita, sandblasted to whiteness, defines active lines in space, accented here with pale yellow blooms of 'Kindly Light' hemerocallis. Chartreuse yucca spears flare vertically from the Norma Olsen porcelain, celadon enriched by poured gray glaze. The branch is simply hooked to a bronze candleholder.

32

4

Techniques for joining and supporting

No matter how beautiful the wood, if it is not securely placed in a design, you are in for disappointment. I learned this in that elementary school of trial and error. To help you avoid my mistakes, here are some of the mechanics for holding wood firmly in place, alone or with other materials.

First an emphatic *don't* try to hammer a nail into a piece of weathered wood. More likely than not it will shatter. It is hard to tell what sections are fragile, and the stress of a hammer blow may prove fatal.

TOOLS AND MATERIALS

All my equipment is small and easy to handle. I do the necessary cleaning and carpentry myself—the cutting, drilling, and
joining. The procedures are relatively simple. Tools for
cleaning include a garden *hose,* fine and heavy *wire brushes,*
a *bottle-brush, toothbrush,* and a soft *scrubbing brush.*

For cutting, I use a sharp *keyhole saw* with fine teeth on
one edge and coarse on the other. This saw is useful for
delicate and heavy pieces. A small *knife* is kept well sharpened
for removing twigs and nubs, and for scraping.

A *small electric hand drill* with bits from $\frac{1}{16}$ to $\frac{1}{4}$ inch
is essential for making holes in bases and weathered pieces.
For cutting metal coat-hangers into pins or dowels, I use a
wire cutter. Other equipment includes: a *hacksaw* for solid
metal rods, which come in lengths up to three feet; *screws*
and a *screw driver* to join sections; *wood-filler, sandpaper,*
and *pastel chalks, stains, paint* or *Liquidtex* to conceal the
screws; and a *propane torch* for burning sodium silicate
(water glass) to a crusty white texture—a technique dis-
cussed in Chapter 3.

For the designs themselves I depend upon: *needlepoint
holders* and *cup needlepoints* that can be filled with water;
plastic tubes to hold water for fresh materials, and I prefer
plastic to glass tubes because plastic is lighter and can be
drilled at the top and pinned to the wood; and *pushpins,
corsage,* or other strong *pins* to hold the tubes securely.

TO JOIN WOOD

Several methods can be used for attaching wood to a base
or to other pieces of wood. You need to consider whether the
construction is to be permanent or temporary.

For permanent placement, drill holes for screws just deep

enough to hold them temporarily in place. Then fasten them with a screw driver. This way the screws join sections securely. Delicate pieces sometimes split if you try to screw them together without drilling holes first. And heavier sections are easier to join if a partial hole is drilled. The size, length, and thickness of the screws depend on the size of the pieces being attached.

To keep these mechanics hidden, sink the head of the screw below the surface of the wood. Cover with a little wood-filler. When this dries, sand it smooth and level with the surrounding area. Then color with pastel chalk, stain, or paint—whatever matches the wood.

For temporary joints, drill holes ⅛ inch in diameter. You can cut wire from metal coat-hangers into pins just long enough to fit the holes, insert the pins, and press the two sections of wood together. Heavier pieces take ¼-inch rods and corresponding holes. Don't let the rods show; joined wood is meant to look like a single unit. These mechanics are demonstrated in Figure 13.

A NOTE ON WOOD DOWELS

I do not like to use wood dowels for temporary attachments. For the most part, they are not strong enough unless they are at least ¼-inch diameter, and often a hole that wide cannot be drilled in the wood. Dowels need to be fitted very tight to hold, which makes it almost impossible to pull doweled sections apart. This presents a problem if you are transporting a large piece to an exhibition; taking it in sections is much simpler. If the wood can tolerate a hole large enough for a wood dowel, it is better to make permanent attachments, and glue the dowel in place.

36

BASES

To attach weathered wood to a wooden base requires drilling. Then either screw the piece directly to the base or secure a metal rod through both base and wood. In some designs, I elevate the wood on $\frac{1}{4}$-inch rods of varied lengths, which I may or may not leave exposed.

Bases can be fashioned from smaller pieces of weathered wood—sometimes removed from a large piece—or from blocks of wood cut from a railroad tie or from a section found at a building-supplier. Drill a block in the exact center; then it is easier to balance the wood. If the hole is off center, you only add to the challenge. Insert a metal rod of the right diameter to fit the hole. Then hold the weathered piece in various positions on the rod to determine balance and design. Consider the visual as well as the actual weight of the piece.

When you settle on a satisfactory position, mark the spot on the wood. Drill the wood, making the hole the right diameter to fit the rod already in the base. A *tight* fit is most important.

If you find you have drilled the weathered wood in the wrong place, plug the hole with wood-filler. When the filler dries, smooth it with fine sandpaper and touch it up with coloring material, such as pastel chalk. Too much drilling may weaken the wood, so make your decision with care.

Bases can be made of plaster-of-Paris or an equal mixture of white sand and Portland cement. Add water and stir well before pouring into a mold. For molds, use milk or cottage-cheese cartons or plastic containers. Before pouring in plaster or cement, put stones in the bottom to give weight and stability. While pouring, hold a metal rod in the center until the plaster or cement sets. For best results, let a base dry overnight before you cut away the mold.

Folds in milk cartons may make the bottom of the base uneven. Use a knife to shave away excess plaster. Finish the base with spray or paint, if that is compatible with the design you are making. Otherwise, leave it white or gray.

Bases made of plaster or cement chip easily. They can be a problem if your design is to be moved about. Handle them carefully and keep pastel chalks on hand for emergency touching up.

TALL CONTAINERS

Devising ways to anchor wood in a tall vase can be quite challenging. If the wood has a projection or "finger" that can be stuck inside or hooked over the rim, you may be able to balance it without special means. If not, one solution is to drill a hole, ⅛-inch diameter, vertically in the side of the wood that will rest against the container. Insert a piece of wire that thickness (you can cut it from a metal coat-hanger) in the hole; make it the length of the container. Put the wire inside the vase, as shown in Figure 16; if necessary, bend it over the edge for additional support. Then place other plant material in the vase, which will also help to anchor the wood. Small stones in the vase can be used to weight it.

LOW BOWLS

Some wood is soft enough for you to impale it on a needle-point holder. You can then place holder and wood in a shallow container. Two or three short twigs stuck onto the holder around the wood increase stability.

38

For hard pieces of wood—and many are far too unyielding to fasten by impaling—drill vertically into the part of the wood that will rest in the bowl. Then drill a hole into the center of a small pinholder. Screw the pinholder upside down onto the wood. (Figure 14 shows this technique.) Place a larger pinholder right-side up in the bowl, and lock the pins of the small holder into it. A design using this method is pictured in Figure 18, where the holder is concealed by a small "mespah rose"—a woody burl-shaped growth of mistletoe and the host plant combined in a form suggesting a rose.

To keep wood from absorbing too much water in a bowl, wax or spray the wood with clear plastic. However, I do not feel this is really necessary. I enjoy the effect of water on weathered wood as an element in a design with fresh flowers.

FRESH MATERIALS

If you plan to include fresh flowers and foliage in an arrangement, and a vase with water is not an aspect of your design, there are several ways to provide water. You can condition flowers first by placing stems in deep warm water for several hours or overnight. Heavy foliages, such as rhododendron, laurel, and narrow-leaved evergreens can be submerged in cool water for several hours ahead of time. Then you can use these materials for a brief period in a design without water. Flowers and leaves handled this way should be tested beforehand to determine how well they will last.

With plastic flower tubes you have a water supply for fresh materials. These tubes are pointed, and you can fit them into crevices or drilled openings in the wood. Or you can drill a hole near the rim of the tube and pin it to the wood. This is shown in Figure 14 and I used it in Figure 15, and in many other designs in this book. Since glass tubes cannot be drilled I do not generally use them in driftwood arrangements.

Cup needlepoint holders set on a level section of wood, secured if necessary with Cling, a floral clay, make it possible to have stems in water. Soaked Oasis, wrapped in foil or plastic, can be used in some designs, as in Figures 21 and 22.

13   Rods cut with wire cutters from metal coat-hangers join sections of driftwood or attach them to bases. First drill holes long enough to hold the wire rods, then put units together. Large composite pieces attached by this method can be dismantled for transporting or storage.

40

14   Tricks of the trade are shown here. From the left, a pinholder-cup for fresh flowers set in a "mespah rose"—a decorative mistletoe burl; weathered wood, drilled and supported on a rod set in a polished wood base, and a small section to join with coat-hanger wire; plastic tube for water pinned to wood set on a rod and base; upside-down needle-point holder screwed to wood to lock into pins of a larger holder that is inside the bronze candlestick; and a grapevine anchored in hollow bamboo sections in a tall pottery container.

42

15   An intricate section of polished roots, brown with an orange glow, holds fresh orange-red 'Tropicana' roses and a bouquet of dried purple statice. Pinned to the wood is a plastic tube (shown in Figure 14) with water for the roses. A metal rod, inserted in holes drilled in a lamp base and through the root, supports the design in space.

44

16   A natural projection anchors the wood in the tall container. On the right, wire inserted in a drilled hole in the wood holds it across the vase in a horizontal position.

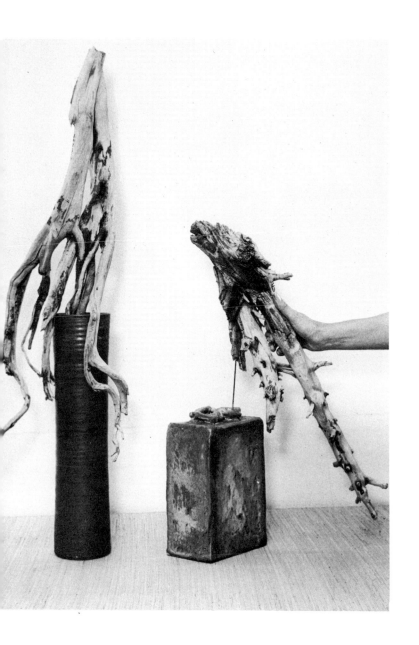

17   A tall container with a long narrow neck is a good choice for wood with natural projections. In this design a piece of the manzanita branch fits down into the Japanese bronze, and 'Limelight' gladiolus contribute stability. Because the wood is securely balanced, delicate linear activity can be freely displayed in space that is well away from the container and the column of green florets.

48

18   Golden umbellatum lilies and a knotted branch of weathered grape vine are anchored by a needlepoint holder in a low chartreuse bowl. The mechanics are concealed by a small "mespah rose." Fresh flowers are placed to counterbalance the assertive linear movement of the wood.

19   Hollow lengths of bamboo placed in a needlepoint support loops of peeled grape vine, two bright forms of red ginger, and feathery bits of Hawaiian pine and lycopodium. Linear emphasis of the bamboo repeated in the Japanese ceramic, is reinterpreted by twists of vine.

50

20   Orange-red gladiolus and pieces of *Curculigo capi-tulata* foliage are combined here with gray-brown textured wood. A needlepoint, attached upside-down to the base of the wood, as shown in Figure 14, is locked into needles of a cupholder in a bronze candle-stick. Striated foliage relates closely to rhythms in wood and is designed as an extension of it. Water in the cupholder keeps materials fresh.

52

21
and
22

Two blocks of soaked Oasis, placed in plastic-lined pockets in a curved shell of wood, hold lime-green and orange marigolds, zinnias, cherry tomatoes, blackberry clusters, and green-and-white dogwood foliage. A fan of wheat, fastened with masking tape, is supported in Styrofoam, wedged in an opening in the wood. Orange Hungarian wax peppers, impaled on green twigs, complete this summertime design.

54

5

Weathered wood

in contemporary designs

AS SCULPTURE,
LINE, ACCESSORY,
CONTAINER

All weathered wood is three dimensional, but when we select qualities to emphasize in a design, the linear may appear more dominant than the sculptural. Or it may be that the grain, the shimmering patina, or the vibrant rhythm of a piece is the outstanding characteristic. It is important to seek out the essential nature of the wood, then develop a design. The materials you select to combine with the wood will then bring proper emphasis.

How the wood is placed—in vertical, diagonal, or horizontal position—on a table or mantel or supported in space,

V   The muted gold of dried yarrow and the brown woody texture
of dried aspidistra leaves relate harmoniously to a formation of
brown roots rubbed with wax. The base is of plaster molded in a
milk carton and painted a similar shade of brown. A metal rod,
inserted in the plaster before it dried, supports the handsome
wooden framework. Other materials are wired in place.

VI Luminous red heliconia bracts, rimmed with contrasting green, and supported on stout green stalks, are framed by gray driftwood and the gray-green foliage of the bromeliad, *Billbergia decora*. The smooth leathery leaves, barred with silver, curl at the tips repeating the shape of the frame. This design shows how compatible tropical materials and wood can be: where wood ends and foliage begins is purposely obscure, and in this context the inflorescens appear wooden. The dark satiny green glass vase is of appropriately simple design.

VII   A stark geometry of bent, clipped papyrus grass contrasts
effectively with an urn-shaped piece of wood, treated here with
copper powder to give it a blue-green patina. This method of coloring wood draws attention to the surface and emphasizes the flowing
rhythms of the grain. Purple thistles, prickly and compact, intro-
duce a third contrasting form to the design which is completed by
a square blue container.

VIII   Glowing tips of orange tritomas and dotted lines of button-
weed, painted fluorescent orange, combine with a silvery piece of
wood from Assateague Island, off the Virginia coast. The green
brushed-yellow philodendron leaves are trimmed to simple shapes.
The many openings in the ridged ceramic by artist Edna Arnow
support wood, flowers, and weeds in this free-style design.

will also contribute interpretation. Most pieces have more than one position in which they are expressive.

My approach in contemporary designs is to be bold, even to exaggerate. The wood is meant to be seen, not smothered in vegetation, and the design should involve the viewer. The weathered wood that I use is all of good size, as you can judge from its relationship to familiar flowers and foliage. I have not sought out ugliness as a means of commanding attention to the wood. I have tried to make clear statements in which the wood is fully respected.

Weathered wood does not have a right-side-up or an upside-down as most flowers do. It can rest on a surface or appear to move freely in space without looking unnatural. One position will suggest the vitality of growth; another, a fallen tree or shattered branch. Yet naturalism is not necessary. We have great freedom when designing with wood. And it often appears as a piece of sculpture as in Figures 23, 24, 25, 26, 27, 28, 29, and 35.

AS SCULPTURE

As with other kinds of sculpture, except bas-reliefs, a composition with weathered wood should be of interest from all angles. A piece with openings through the wood may recall the sculpture of Barbara Hepworth or Henry Moore, and as Hepworth paints one plane a brilliant blue, we may select an orange anthurium to emphasize dimension through contrast in color.

Sections of weathered wood can be joined into a unified structure with mass predominating, as in Figure 24. While the wood alone is beautiful, we who arrange flowers enjoy creating designs that include fresh materials for the living quality they bring. Whether you select plant material with

57

bold form as a reinterpretation of mass, or delicate, fragile shapes to contrast with it, will depend on your personal feelings. Today we express these feelings directly in our designs. There is hardly a flower, fruit, leaf, or vine that would appear incongruous, or that cannot associate attractively with the once-living wood.

AS LINE

While much of the weathered wood we find is primarily sculptural simply because it is three dimensional, there are pieces with linear emphasis. Thin ends of branches, outer portions of roots, and wood with noticeable grain running the length of it can be used for their linear qualities, as in Figures 30, 31, 32, 33, 34. Any number of roots and vines— corkscrew willow, wisteria, bittersweet, honeysuckle, grape —soaked in water and tied or shaped into outlines, when dry can provide linear material for arrangements.

The position of the wood will contribute to linear emphasis. Branches seen clearly in space or in contrast to solid objects—a container or a floral mass—will appear as lines rather than as volumetric forms. And lighting will add to this effect if well directed.

Because our eyes move in the direction lines establish, they provide motion and rhythm. Whether graceful or dynamic, nervous, urgent, positive, or restful, lines and the spaces between them are of great value in structuring a design.

AS ACCESSORY

When naturalism was important in floral designs, figures frequently contributed to the story or the sense of a mood. As a rule, figures are no longer included in contemporary work. But occasionally a weathered piece suggests an animal, bird, insect, or fish so emphatically that it is not seen as branch or root, or used as an abstract form or for line. One such humorous treasure in my collection is a brown wood "bird" picked up on the bank of the Ohio River (Figure 35).

AS CONTAINER

Almost any piece of weathered wood can serve as container—any shape or size as in Figures 28, 36, 37, 38, and 39. It need not resemble a standard vase or ceramic. The wood may already have a flat section on which you can set a needlepoint cupholder or openings to hold plastic tubes. If not, you can make a level area with saw or knife for a holder. Pieces of wood often have pulpy interiors. Scoop out the rotted part, scrub the hollow with hot water and soap and let dry out completely. Then waterproof with a plastic spray and you will have made a place for a cupholder or dish for water.

Trunks of small trees make excellent containers and usually have soft interiors that are relatively simple to clean out and waterproof. A hollow log once scrubbed may hold a glass or plastic jar. And burls—those rounded knobs that grow on trunks of many trees—make fine low bowls. They are often rotted inside by insects and elements and are easily cleaned. Treated with plastic waterproof spray, they will hold water.

The surface of wood can be treated by any of the methods described in Chapter 4. You can sand the wood and rub it to a soft finish or texture it with a coarse wire brush. For other effects, use stain, oil, wax, chalk, or one of the chemical preparations. The blue-green patina is attractive for many designs.

59

23   To let form dominate, only a few materials are brought to this design. The surging upward movement is punctuated by rounds of lotus pods set on three planes and is extended with andromeda foliage. Contributing more intricate forms are two pieces of embryo palm. Color is subdued, to give emphasis to the deep honey tones of the Lake Michigan wood. Here is an abstraction of the famous statue, Winged Victory, or simply a rhythmic form poised on a dark weathered cube.

60

24   Three sections of wood are temporarily joined and brought into contrast with a geometry of cattails. Sharp angles at the center, swift diagonals, and emphatic points create an excitement that opposes the heavier forms and slower rhythms of the weathered wood. The dark railroad-tie block is repeated in the velvet of reeds, the supporting metal dowel in their tips. Economy in materials draws attention to form and line.

25   The volumetric form of a silvery hornets' nest, embellished with a cluster of 'Red Dot' geraniums and green frilled leaves, is supported by a complex of grape branches. Placing the nest at the top lets the papery mass dominate. Branches are drilled and impaled on a metal dowel set in a weathered block. Geraniums are fastened to a ball of soaked Oasis, wrapped in foil, and placed inside the nest.

62

26   A tree root, decorated with the blue berries and glossy leaves of mahonia, serves as a stand for this sculptured piece. Opposing the symmetry is the diagonal thrust of an orange hemerocallis; a dynamic tension exists between the bright flower and the black void. To keep materials fresh, they are placed in a water-filled plastic tube which is fitted into a groove in the root. A metal dowel supports the wood.

64

27 To display its baroque motion, a deeply grooved, coarse-grained twist of tan manzanita is fastened upright on a metal dowel. Seen as part of the form is a dried desert artichoke of closely associated texture and color. Long-needled Austrian pine enlivens the design with contrasting linear rhythms.

28   A bonelike formation of dark gray wood is mounted
as sculpture on a rod set in a polished black cube.
Below, an irregular sculptural form makes a container for banded lengths of equisetum, which intro-
duces graceful lines. The starkness of the design
lets attention dwell on these fragile-seeming sur-
realistic shapes.

68

29   While emphasis is clearly on the sculptured form of
the wood, outward thrust is tempered by placing the
petals of golden day-lilies against the wood. Subtle
variations in tones and pleasing rhythms in the light
brown root are brought out as well as the three-
dimensional aspect of the design. The uppermost
flower rises as an extension of the wood, not in
opposition to it. Plastic tubes hold water to keep the
day-lilies fresh.

70

30   With the speed of lightning, a bleached manzanita branch provides dramatic rhythms that lead directly to bursts of yellow Dutch iris and the quiet curve of bronze Andorra juniper. Small nervous lines are clearly etched in space, while the heavier diagonal is defined by the cylindrical volume of the hand-thrown Japanese ceramic. Strong direct lighting accentuates the linear aspect of the branch.

72

31   A tracery of angular red locust branches with strong horizontal lines is contrasted with the compact petaled rounds of orange ranunculus. Linear decoration on the white ceramic contributes a tempered vertical. Lines defined by space dominate the arrangement. A needlepoint holds materials at the center, and branches are interlocked.

32   Roots gathered along a stream establish the quiet rhythms of this design. Peeled and placed in a sinuous vertical curve, the smooth wood interacts with prickly branches and long-needled clusters and cones of Scotch pine. A dried artichoke center brings a puff of orange to complement the green.

76

33   Lines of manzanita, defined in space, contrast with a colorful textured mass. The container, a rococo shell-shaped "mespah rose," supports orange-berried pyracantha branches with leaves. The fresh pineapple is held in the cup needlepoint. The stout loop of manzanita creates emphatic rhythm that leads the eye down through the design, then out and upward to more delicate lines and the spaces they describe. The branch is anchored to the "rose" by a metal pin that passes through holes drilled in both. A cupholder of water keeps the pyracantha fresh.

78

34   In this design flowers are given prominence while the wood provides a strong but subdued rhythmic frame. The bright white-petaled Shasta daisies with yellow centers are set off by leathery dark green Carolina rhododendron leaves. Inside the mustard-colored ceramic, by Edna Arnow, a block of Oasis holds daisies and foliage. One of the pottery loops contributes support to the wood.

80

35　　Carved and shaped by the elements, this long-necked "fowl" needed only to be set on a pedestal of gnarled roots to be seen for what it is. In this setting of garden alliums and hosta leaves, it crows vigorously. A metal pin in drilled holes joins the two sections of wood, and a cupholder with water supports fresh materials.

36   A tall curved shell of dark gray wood, anchored by
      a metal rod on a polished cube, serves as container
      for tangerine carnations, purple clematis, and
      bronze mahonia. A cupholder on a leveled area inside
      the top keeps this cascade of flowers fresh.

      84

37   A hollow log with barnacle projections has been
drilled to hold stems and rod attached to a brown
lamp base. To suggest a wallpaper pattern or display
dried materials for botanical study, pods and grasses
have been inserted in the holes.

86

38   This handsome double trunk with two natural openings has been waxed and polished to a glowing finish. Needlepoint cupholders in each opening support Austrian pine, rose-colored ginger, green tufts of papyrus, and tan palm ribbons in a design of contrasting textures.

39   A gourd, mottled orange, tan, and brown, provides an unusual container that suggests an early Tiffany design. Red and pink roses, compactly placed, are shown in contrast to the delicate lines and pointed leaves of a pruned Japanese maple branch.

90

6

New associations

DESIGNS
FOR THE HOLIDAYS
AND THE SEASONS

In interpretations with wood for holidays and other occasions, we often want to use materials of traditional association. Because of its great versatility, we discover that weathered wood is compatible with lilies for Easter, tree ornaments for Christmas, fruits for Thanksgiving, candles for the New Year. Seasonal arrangements for spring, summer, fall, and winter can also be developed, and free-form or abstract designs that are subject to any interpretation come easily with wood.

The designs here are intended to illustrate the scope and

freedom that wood offers. Weathered wood can also associate appropriately with garden flowers—fresh or dried, as daisies and sunflowers; with exotic anthuriums and billbergias; with lilies, iris, and chrysanthemums from the florist; mullein from the wild; broad- and narrow-leaved evergreens; as well as with the berries of mountain ash and viburnum, catalpa "beans" and grape clusters. In this chapter and, indeed, throughout this book are shown the many aspects of nature that can be correlated with wood—and the infinite variety in weathered wood, itself.

40   For Easter, two branches of manzanita, lightened by sandblasting, bring delicate linear movement above and below three satin-white regal lilies, interpretative of the Trinity. The smooth, angular, black polished forms of the metal container and base afford subdued contrast, softened by the dark pointed leaves.

92

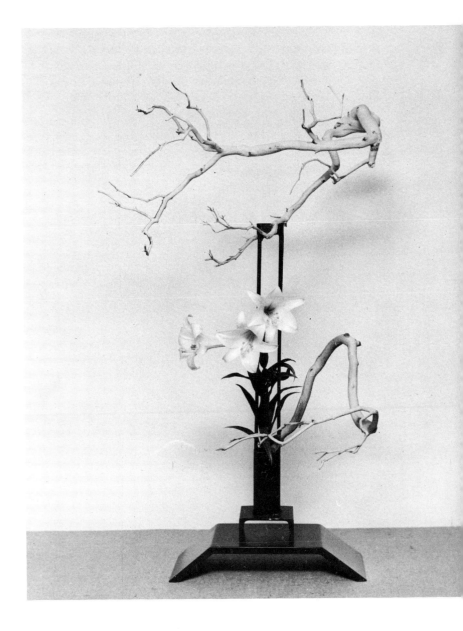

41   A sheaf of pale wheat, a yellow "football" chrysanthemum, a cluster of green, purple, and black grapes, and a ceramic mallard duck—traditional elements of the harvest season—are brought into new association with a coarse-textured piece of red-brown wood from Holton, Michigan. A needlepoint holder set in the mustard-glazed, Japanese, free-form container supports the wood in a bold upright position, and a plastic tube holds water for the flower.

42 A length of gray, bleached wood moves rhythmically and emphatically up through a massed design of dark green Japanese yew, pungent bayberry branches, and shining magnolia leaves placed in a dark green cylinder. Providing lively accents are the clusters of waxy gray-white bayberries, which are frequently made into spicy candles to burn at Christmastime.

43   Three sections of gray wood with shadings of brown are joined by wood dowels to make a pedestaled crescent on a black polished base. For a holiday decoration, blue and green Christmas ornaments—the wire stems twisted together and tucked among the greens—and branches of blue-green juniper are placed to follow the curves of the wood.

44   In holiday red and green, long thin green "beans" from a catalpa tree dangle in sprightly seesaw on a fulcrum of red gladiolus, yellow and orange-red viburnum berries, and a stout piece of whitened wood. A slab-built moss-green ceramic signed by a Canadian artist, Marks, has two irregular openings to support wood in front and gladiolus in back. Pods are pinned and berries draped over the catalpa branches.

45   A single complicated piece of smooth brown and
gray wood with arresting diagonal movement holds
a festive display of pods, cones, and foliages appropriate to holiday decorating. A tall curved tuft
of coconut palm is anchored to the wood by a metal
rod. Pine, mahonia, holly, piñon cones, and lotus
pods are tied with wire, and the footed amber hob-
nail candle-cups are set in holes drilled in the wood.

46   Reddish brown textured wood with a rope of roots
      enclosing space, is boldly enlivened with curved
      stems of dried mullein, painted fluorescent orange,
      and a peeled sunflower head, sprayed hot pink.
      Floral tape and natural openings support these ma-
      terials in fanciful iconoclasm.

47   In a more traditional expression, fresh yellow forsythia and Dutch iris are displayed with an elegant fluted "mespah rose," which holds a needlepoint cup. These spring flowers associate charmingly with the woody mistletoe burl container. Similar to more common burls or lichens, "mespah roses" are found in Mexico on trees on which parasitic mistletoe grows.

48   Sweeping lengths of the curly tipped leaves of *Bill-bergia decora,* and pointed gray ironwood form an angle, which is embellished by pink gladiolus, and pink-and-red croton leaves. One section of wood fits into the mottled Japanese bronze and provides support for flowers and foliage. These are kept fresh in Oasis soaked and wrapped in foil. Above, a cluster of gray billbergia pods contributes texture.

49   Two rhythmic sections of tan manzanita are joined by a metal dowel to make one dynamic unit. Curled bronze ti leaves accentuate the upward thrust, and bright orange anthuriums contribute motion and color. With weathered wood and just a few plant materials a forceful design can be achieved in contemporary manner.

108

50   A rhythmic, sinuous twisting root runs like a cord the length of this design, and encloses two spatial areas that counterbalance the giant brown-ribbed, white cecropia leaf and the dried yarrow cushions, which are accented with cedar. A bronze-green cylinder supports the wood; the dried materials are pressed into twists in the root.

51   An elegant, sculptured section of gray wood with subtle folds and soft patina seems to revolve on an armature of metal rod and black-lacquered weed. Balancing the "stabile" are spiny bronze mahonia leaves and a colorful cluster of red geraniums and blue mahonia berries, both set in a plastic tube.

52   Bold assertive rhythms begin with baroque twists of manzanita, used as a base, move through rounds of dried peeled beige sunflower heads and dark brown desert artichokes to a corded plume of coconut palm. Stems are placed in holes drilled in the wood, and the palm is attached by a metal rod that runs through lotus pod and wood. Form and motion are emphasized in this monochromatic design.

53   A single section of lightweight, almost white, wood is hung horizontally as a wall decoration for Christmastime. Scarlet mountain-ash berries and spears of split okra pods, wired to form clusters, embellish one end of the wood. Different materials can be used for other occasions, while the wood remains firmly in place.

54   Weathered boards from a demolished barn serve as appropriate backing for a plaque of driftwood and fresh and dried plant material to be hung as a picture. The gray wood has been painted turkey-red and toned down with umber. Screws secure driftwood permanently to the boards. Lotus, poppy, and baptisia pods, "mespah roses," desert artichokes, and lichen are wired to the driftwood, permitting change of materials. Orange-red mountain-ash berries are fresh and held only by strong stems. Plastic tubes, wedged between wood and pods, would keep any flowers fresh.

116

55   By placing two lemon hemerocallis flowers and buds, without customary length of stem to separate them from the massive gray wood, a new sense of scale is achieved—the flowers appear large in relation to the wood. A bundle of stems brings diagonal excitement as do the cattail reeds, which move into an opening in the wood in spatial interplay.

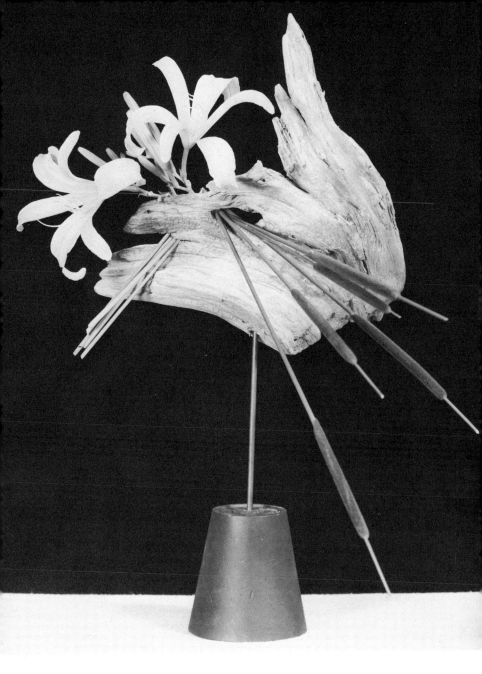

IX   This reinterpretation of line-mass designing presents a com-
bination of fresh, dried, weathered, and contrived materials. At the
top, a dried cecropia leaf folds into a silver round supported on a
line of root. Fresh green grapes associate with pecan nuts, individ-
ually wrapped in nylon stocking and wired to form a grapelike
cluster, the mechanics concealed by brown floral tape. Brown-pink
croton leaves are kept fresh in a plastic tube and a rod inserted
in a weathered cube of wood supports the compact brown burl.

X A festive bouquet of red geraniums, with a few green geranium
leaves and clipped branches of waxy bayberry, is contained in a
hollowed burl, attached by screws to a tripod of weathered branch.
Both brown burl and gray branch are rubbed with gray pastel
chalk. Curved, dried, elaeagnus branches describe graceful elipses
in space, reinterpreting the burl in this holiday design.

XI Bleached weathered wood, here a wall ornament, is drama-
tized by a strong diagonal of long-stemmed golden daisy chrysanthemums and dark brown cattails, these drawn through a natural
opening in the wood and pinned in place. A concealed water-filled
plastic tube keeps flowers fresh, and they can be replaced by others,
wood and cattails remaining a permanent aspect of this study in
special relationships, and the cluster of red berries making a
long-lasting accent.

XII For Christmas holidays, a compact burl, with an S-shaped
section joined to it, is decorated with traditional evergreens—
holly, juniper, spruce—piñon cones, and shining ornaments. A
metal rod in the brown-painted plaster-of-Paris base securely holds
the wood high above the festive display.

Guides for point-scoring
designs with weathered wood

For a holiday
    Communication   40
    Textural
      relationships   20
    Creativity   25
    Technique   15
               100

With flowers
    Association of
      all materials   25
    Design   30
    Creative quality   35
    Condition   10
               100

As sculpture
    Suitability of
      form   35
    Balance   25
    Expression   25
    Distinction   15
               100

With roadside materials
    Design   45
    Personal
      expression   30
    Technique   15
    Condition   10
               100

With dried materials
- Design 30
- Color 25
- New approach 30
- Distinction 15

  100

In space
- Spatial balance 40
- Freshness of concept 35
- Distinction 25

  100

Expression of line or lines
- Design 30
- Linear aspects 20
- Association of all materials 25
- Distinction 25

  100

As an accessory
- Appropriateness 20
- Design 40
- Personal expression 25
- Technique 15

  100

With exotic materials
- Design 30
- Association of all materials 35
- Creativity 25
- Condition 10

  100

122

Using treated materials
Conformance to
   schedule 15
Color expression 25
Technique 15
Association of all
   materials 15
Design 30
          100

Flowers and vegetables
Design 30
Texture 25
Color 20
Distinction 25
      100

Flowers and fruits
Association of
   all materials 15
Design 30
New approach 35
Distinction 20
      100

Fruits and vegetables
Design 20
Association of
   all materials 30
Color 20
Expression 30
      100

Index

Weathered Wood with Flowers by Mary G. Knight
Illustrations are indicated by heavy type.

124

125

127

ABOUT THE AUTHOR

Mary G. Knight (in private life Mrs. John W. Knight, Jr., mother of two sons and grandmother of six boys and girls), is an accredited instructor of flower arrangement and flower show practice for the National Council. Her lectures and demonstrations have delighted and informed audiences in some twenty states, beside her native Ohio. She has also been repeatedly invited to demonstrate for clubs in Canada. Her lectures cover many subjects, especially contemporary free-form and abstract designs, table settings, Christmas decorations, Oriental styles, and, of course, her favorite weathered wood.

Mrs. Knight has been president of many garden-club groups and has been the recipient of many honors—winner of the $5,000 trophy awarded in the 1958 Sterling Bowl Tournament, sponsored by the Jackson & Perkins Company, and in 1966 the National Council Helen S. Hull Award for an outstanding calendar arrangement. Mrs. Knight makes frequent T.V. appearances and is the author of ABSTRACT AND NOT-SO ABSTRACT FLOWER ARRANGEMENT.